Please, thank you, welcome, YEAH!

"And by the way, birds don't have butts!"

Audra Dean

WestBow Press books may be ordered through booksellers or by contacting:

WestBow Press
A Division of Thomas Nelson & Zondervan
1663 Liberty Drive
Bloomington, IN 47403
www.westbowpress.com
844-714-3454

ISBN: 979-8-3850-1291-6 (sc)
ISBN: 979-8-3850-1292-3 (e)

Library of Congress Control Number: 2023922277

Print information available on the last page.

WestBow Press rev. date: 02/21/2024

WESTBOW
PRESS®
A DIVISION OF THOMAS NELSON
& ZONDERVAN

September 5, 2023

My book of Evanisms

This book is dedicated to my cousin Bonnie who passed away the evening of September 17, 2023. She fought a lifelong battle with something called CMT-1, which is a muscular dystrophy of sorts and at the age of 60 was also diagnosed with end stage Parkinson's disease. When I went back to my home state to sit with her I asked her what I could do for her. She said all she wanted was love and laughter. Well, I provided both and took my "Evanisms" up to Wyoming and read them to her. We laughed so hard she needed to use her inhaler to catch her breath. I knew then and there that I would come back to Colorado and finish writing and dedicate it to her. Fly high Ms. Bonnie Bulow Tierney—until we meet again!

We started calling the funny things our boy said "Evanisms" early on. I have two very smart, talkative, and articulate children. I think it's because their momma talks. And talks. And talks. And talks, some more. From about 18 months old Evan spoke in full sentences and rarely needed us to translate for him when speaking to someone he had just met. Some of the things that came out of and still do come out of his mouth are downright hysterical. I pray you get as much joy and laughter out of our "Evanisms" as we have over the years.

I am an RN and used to work nightshifts every other weekend. One of these weekends I asked a fouryear-old Evan what he thought he and daddy would do today. "I don't know mom. Probably poop and then go fishing."

Potty training was a lot of fun with this kid

Me: Evan go potty before bed, please.

Evan: but I don't have to mom.

Me: please go try

Evan: but moooooommmmmm

Me: GO!!

Evan: OK!!!

Me: Did you go?

Evan: I tried, but nothing came out because it's not loaded!!

When Evan was 4 he got a new pair of shoes. They were Sketchers with memory foam. Driving to gymnastics and he yells "Wow, mom these really work! I just remembered something I had forgotten!"

At age 4 Evan used to call his snowpants a super funny name. They had the pants plus the straps that go over the shoulders. One morning after watching the news and seeing all the snow people in Colorado had gotten, he insisted he had to go play in the little skiff of snow we did get. I told him buddy; we didn't get all the snow everyone on the news got. "But mommmmmmm. I need my snowveralls so I can go play in the snow!!"

When Evan was at his 4 year well child check his doctor referred to him as "spirited." I am pretty sure that was code for "wow this kid is out of control!" So when he misbehaved after that we would just laugh and say look how "spirited" he is being.

Also at the age of 4, he wasn't quiet when he made observations. Like the time we walked into our hotel lobby just as group of people were heading back to their room and Evan not so quietly says "hey there's all the old people headed back from the pool!"

One night at the dinner table my husband says "the neighbors move out Friday. They sold their house to a large Russian family" Evan says: "Just like us!" I was confused and said "Evan, we aren't Russian!" and he says:" Mom, we are ALWAYS Russian around, Russian here, Russian there!"

Evan made a flower in preschool with the help of his teacher for Mother's Day when he was 4. It had questions written on the petals and his answers were written on the backs of them.

What does your mom do all day? She sleeps all day and she doesn't eat lunch (in my defense I was a nightshift nurse)

What does she do at work? She is a doctor and takes care of babies in the PICU

Where is her favorite place to go? The new house

What makes her sad? She doesn't get sad (favorite answer)

What is she not so good at? Getting up (least favorite see above nightshift nurse)

What do you do together? Watch the news (most confusing answer)

One night while I was at work my husband was stretching on the floor and flopped his arms back and closed his eyes. Evan forgot the first step of CPR being "daddy daddy are you ok?" and started CPR with full on breaths and compressions and when Troy sat up Evan yelled "I SAVED YOU!!" Truly sorry I missed that.

While playing doctor with the kids I'm thinking to myself these kids have no clue what they're doing! Evan was the nurse and his sister Kaia was the doctor and I was the patient. I was "asleep" for surgery and then when they woke me up they said they had replaced my liver. Turns out they did know what they were doing, I probably needed a new liver.

Troy: "It's raining, it's pouring"
Evan: "Dad is annoying!" he was the ripe old age of 5

Evan was a very good reader from early on (thank you Ms. Melissa) but would obviously get tripped up on larger words. At age 5, listening to satellite radio and he wanted to know if the band singing Jet City Woman was called Queens crotch.

You have to know your 6 year old watches too much TV when he comes down the stairs and asks if his 10 year old sister suffers from urinary incontinence!

Me: "Evan, not everything you think needs to come out of your mouth!" Evan: "You want it to come out my rear end?"

Evan's grandfather Roger moved in with us after we had just gotten a hedgehog for a pet. Evan informed Roger that Piper would be a little skittish around him for awhile because she had never seen a senior citizen before.

Evan was singing Cheeseburger in Paradise by the late Jimy Buffet and so I asked him what's paradise Evan?

Evan: "It's a couple things you shake and roll." Pair o dice!

Evan went into the locker room at the pool at our timeshare and came back out with deodorant on. He said it was to make his armpit farts smell good.

When Evan was 2 he got to spend lots of time with his great auntie Linda as she watched him while I slept in between nightshifts and my husband worked days. He told her one day that if she got cousin Michael some new Nike shoes like his he could run really really fast too. (Mikey was in a wheelchair unable to walk since birth)

Daddy said to Evan "love you Evan"

Evan says "I love you too (two) daddy! No wait, I love you one. It's better than two!"

Evan was 3 and loved looking at junk mail and pretending he was reading it. One particular afternoon after my parents had been down to visit he was flipping through the magazine Troy had given him and he shakes his head and says "Silly politicians!" Thanks Papa Perry

Also at the age of two he politely asked "Mom, can I please watch something on the TV that is appropriate for me to watch?

One of my all time favorites (now, not then) came two days before turning three. Troy asked

"Evan when are you going to start listening to mommy and daddy? Why don't you listen to us?" Evan: "Mostly because you guys don't know what you're talking about!"

Not to be outdone by "Evan—when are you going to start listening to mommy and daddy?

You're 4 now!"

Evan: "I don't know, I was thinking like 5 or 6?"

Evan has always been the type of kid that doesn't want to be told he should or shouldn't do something and does things on his own timeline. He was exactly three years old when he decided to potty train. A few days after his third birthday and he and Troy were at Walmart shopping for big kid underwear and Troy said to him "we will have to ask someone where your size underwear is. There are none right here. So Evan not so politely tells the store worker "this is ridiculous you don't have any underwear my size. We're going to Target!"

Thankfully, this next Evanism comes after potty training. "Mommy, I am pooping a lot! I am sir poops a lot!"

Yelling from the bathroom "Mommy, I am done pooping!"

Me: "You're sure you're done?"

Evan: "I'm done. I'm done!"

Me: "Did you just toot?"

Evan: "Yep, mom, I just tooted a rainbow!"

Troy asked Evan for kisses and Evan said "I can't, kisses are out of your network!"

Still only three years old and using huge words. He was messing around in his room and somehow got stuck behind the door of his room. When Troy went to check on him he says "Well this is a peculiar predicament I've gotten myself into, Busted!"

Kindergarten assignment If I were president....I would fire everyone
It's a wonder the kid learned to spell and read so well with the help
he received from one of his parents. Troy told Evan he could have
dessert if he could spell it and then promptly helped him spell desert.

"One pea stuck to another pea=peepee and by the way birds don't have rear ends" quote from three year old Evan

Not to be outdone by a three-year-old that starts a sentence with "well mom, the truth is..."

Lots of potty humor with a small boy it seems...He got up one particular night yelling "I have to poop!!" He goes into the bathroom and does his business and comes out saying "I named that one Mario, because it came out fast!"

This one is also a favorite and shows his sense of humor so very well

Me: "Evan, go to bed."

Evan: "But I have to pee." Done

Me: "Evan, go to bed."

Evan: "But I need a drink." Done

Me: "Evan, go to bed."

Evan: "But I need hugs and kisses. From everyone!" Done

Me: "Evan, go to bed!!!!"

Evan: "But mom, I have to ask you a question."

Me: "NOW WHAT???"

Evan: "How much wood would a woodchuck chuck if a woodchuck could chuck wood?"

While looking at a catalogue for birthday presents for his 4th birthday he asks "mom, am I three and up or three and down?"

Right before his 5th birthday he came out of my closet with a boppy pillow around his neck and says "Hey, I found my neck pillow!" I said "baby that's where you used to lay when I fed you as a baby" and patted my chest. A look of shear disgust comes across his face and he says "Why didn't you just put it in a cup for me???"

Still very witty at the ripe old age of 10 on April 30th, 2020 (yep, pandemic humor)

Me: "You hear that son? You're not likely to get or spread the Rona! But don't go lick carts at Walmart"

Evan: "Well, there goes my plans for Friday!!"

Evan: "There's no popsicles in the freezer!"

Troy: "There's a pacifist in the freezer? Why?"

Evan: "I don't know dad, cuz he didn't fight back??"

Printed in the United States
by Baker & Taylor Publisher Services